Contents

Royal Children   4

The Lonely Princess   6

The Teen Queen   8

Queen Victoria's Children   10

'Poor Bertie': Edward VII   12

The Second Son: George V   14

The Shy Prince   16

'Lilibet'   18

Princess Elizabeth   20

Future King: Prince Charles   22

The People's Prince: William   24

Party Prince: Harry   26

Life After Childhood   28

Glossary   30

Websites/Timeline   31

Index   32

Royal Children

Future Kings, George VI (left) and Edward VIII (right), dressed in their swimsuits.

It's easy to imagine that a royal childhood is privileged, charmed and carefree. While it's true young royals spend their time in palaces with nannies and servants, their lives are not always as easy as you think.

Queen Victoria's father died when she was a baby, and she was raised by a mother who always felt like an outsider. Her son, Edward VII, was bullied by his father. George V and George VI battled shyness. Elizabeth II seems to be the first of our monarchs to have had a happy childhood.

This book takes a look at the true stories of some British royal children from 1819 to today. On pages 28–29 you can find out what happened to them when they grew up, and there is a timeline on page 31 that puts their lives in context.

"We are a member of the British royal family. We are never tired, and we all love hospitals."

Queen Mary, mother of Edward VIII and George VI

A ROYAL Childhood

200 years of Royal babies

Liz Gogerly

W

FRANKLIN WATTS

LONDON • SYDNEY

First published in 2013 by Franklin Watts

Copyright © Franklin Watts 2013

Franklin Watts
338 Euston Road
London NW1 3BH

Franklin Watts Australia
Level 17/207 Kent Street
Sydney, NSW 2000

A CIP catalogue record for this book
is available from the British Library.

Dewey number: 941'.0099

ISBN
Hardback: 978 1 4451 2669 2
E-book: 978 1 4451 2670 8
Library E-book: 978 1 4451 2686 9

Printed in China

Franklin Watts is a division of Hachette Children's Books, an Hachette UK company.

www.hachette.co.uk

Editor: Sarah Ridley
Editor in Chief: John C. Miles
Designer: Jason Billin
Art director: Peter Scoulding
Picture research: Diana Morris

Picture credits: Bobey100/istockphoto: 14br. Dan Breckwold/Shutterstock: 12b. Central Press/Getty Images: 22b. Classic Image/Alamy: front cover tr, 7. Michael Foley/Dreamstime: 15t. The Granger Collection/Topfoto: 13. Andrew Howe/istockphoto: 9cr. Hulton Archive/Getty Images: 5tr, 18t, 19t. Image Management Asset/Superstock: 12t. Interfoto/Alamy: 6t. Ian Jones/St James's Palace/Topfoto: 25bl. Keystone Pictures USA/Alamy: back cover c, 29t. Brendan MacRae/Getty Images: front cover tl, back cover br, 1, 19b. Mary416/Shutterstock: 6bl. National Pictures/Topfoto: 24t PA Photos/Topfoto, front cover bl, 5b, 22t, 24b, 25t, 26b, 27b. Picturepoint/Topham: 4, 11b, 16t, 17bl, 17r, 21t, 23bl. Ivan Ponomarev/istockphoto: front cover tc. Print Collector/HIP/Topfoto: front cover cl & cr, 16b, 18b. Lisa Sheridan/Getty Images: 20b, 23br. Sulky/Shutterstock: front cover background. Topfoto: 10, 14t, 28. Topical Press Agency/Getty Images: 21b. UPP/Topfoto: 27t.

Unexpected Duties

Many of the monarchs of the past two hundred years were not expected to become king or queen: Victoria, George V, George VI and Elizabeth II.

Elizabeth II has successfully ruled over the country for over sixty years. Her son, Charles, has had plenty of time to learn how to be a king, but will he ever be crowned? Some people think his son William may be our next king.

> *"* It's all to do with the training: you can do a lot if you're properly trained. *"* *Elizabeth II*

King George VI when Duke of York with his wife, Elizabeth. He became king when his brother, Edward VIII, abdicated.

Child in the Camera

The British people have watched Prince William grow up from a baby (left). Many people felt his grief when his mother died. His marriage was watched by millions of people, who will be equally interested in following his own family as they grow up.

The Lonely Princess

When Alexandrina Victoria was born on 24 May 1819 the bells didn't ring out nor did the newspapers go wild. The plump baby girl was fifth in line to the throne and most people didn't expect her to be queen one day.

Princess Victoria (Drina to the family) was born and grew up at Kensington Palace in London. Victoria's father, the Duke of Kent, was the fourth son of George III, and died when she was eight months old. Victoria's mother, the Duchess of Kent, was German and often felt out of place in English society.

Home Alone

Victoria was an only child and life was quiet and lonely. Her mother's close friend Sir John Conroy was employed as comptroller of the household. Sir John believed that Victoria would be the Queen one day and he attempted to control the life of the princess, hoping to be her private secretary in time.

Victoria, aged two, with her mother, the Duchess of Kent.

Sir John Conroy, whom Victoria disliked intensely.

Kensington Palace, Victoria's childhood home, is still a royal palace today.

Horrid House Rules

It was Sir John that came up with a strict daily routine for Victoria called the 'Kensington system'. Rules included being made to sleep in her mother's bedroom. Meals were simple and included a lot of bread and milk. Cups of tea were a luxury.

Like many upper-class girls at the time, Victoria was educated at home by a governess, Baroness Louise Lehzen. She recorded Victoria's attitude and learning in 'behaviour books'. On 1 November 1831 Victoria's behaviour is described as "VERY, VERY, VERY, VERY HORRIBLY NAUGHTY!"

Happy Times

Later in life Victoria described her childhood as 'dreary'. It wasn't all doom and gloom in the Kensington household though. Victoria loved horse riding and her little dog Dash. She was good at drawing and painting. She also had a prized collection of dolls that she enjoyed dressing up.

This portrait shows Princess Victoria as a child aged about 8.

Royal Reads

Victoria didn't read many novels when she was growing up. Instead of reading Jane Austen and other female authors, such as Fanny Burney, the future queen had her nose in history, geography and law books, or the works of poets like Alexander Pope and William Cowper.

The Teen Queen

Victoria's uncle George IV died when Victoria was eleven. King William IV took the throne and the princess became heir. A law was passed to allow Victoria's mother to act as Regent should Victoria become queen while still a child.

Victoria was sixteen and feeling ill when Sir John Conroy tried to get her to sign official papers promising to make him her secretary. Victoria's governess, Baroness Lehzen, was a great support and backed the princess when she refused to sign the document.

The Princess Diaries

The teenage princess blurted out some of her pent-up feelings in a diary. Most early entries are about what she ate and when she went to bed. As the years passed, the princess became more expressive and opinionated. Visitors to Kensington Palace were described in detail – Victoria often commented on 'pretty' women and 'charming' men.

Victoria's spaniel Dash was a loving companion during the teenage years of the princess.

Victoria hits the Internet

In 2012, the year of Elizabeth II's Diamond Jubilee celebrations, the diary of Victoria went online. Users in Britain can enter any date between 1832 and 1901 and view the Queen's entry for that day. http://www.queenvictoriasjournals.org/search/browseByDate.do

The Princess in Love

Caged up at Kensington and rarely mixing with people of her own age, Victoria was ready to fall in love at an early age. It was love at first sight when she met her German cousin Albert, in 1836. As always, she confided in her diary: "Albert is extremely handsome, his hair is about the same colour as mine; his eyes are large and blue, and he has a beautiful nose and a very sweet mouth with fine teeth; but the charm of his countenance is his expression, which is most delightful."

Nearly a month after her eighteenth birthday, on 20 June 1837, Victoria became the Queen. The teen queen moved to Buckingham Palace and took over the serious business of ruling the country.

Princess Victoria, pictured about the time she became Queen at age 18.

This painting of Albert was made around the time of his engagement to Victoria in 1839.

Queen Victoria's Children

Victoria proposed to her handsome cousin Albert in 1839 and the couple were married the following year. The newlyweds were head over heels in love and went on to have a large family together.

Their first child Victoria (Vicky) was born in 1840. Edward came along the following year and became the heir to the throne. Next came Alice, then Alfred, Helena, Louise, Arthur, Leopold and Beatrice (Baby).

Queen Victoria in her coronation robes.

Disgusting Babies!

Victoria apparently hated being pregnant, giving birth, breast-feeding and just about anything to do with tiny babies: "An ugly baby is a very nasty object – and the prettiest is frightful when undressed – till about four months..." She has gained the reputation for being a cold, strict and overbearing mother. Yet, it must have been difficult juggling her life as queen, wife and mother.

In her defence, Victoria did express love and delight in her babies too. In the 1840s she wrote: "It seems like a dream having a child."

Don't mention the 'P' word!

Most Victorian novels did not discuss pregnancy because it was too shocking. George Eliot was one of the first authors to do so in her novel *Adam Bede*, which was published in 1859.

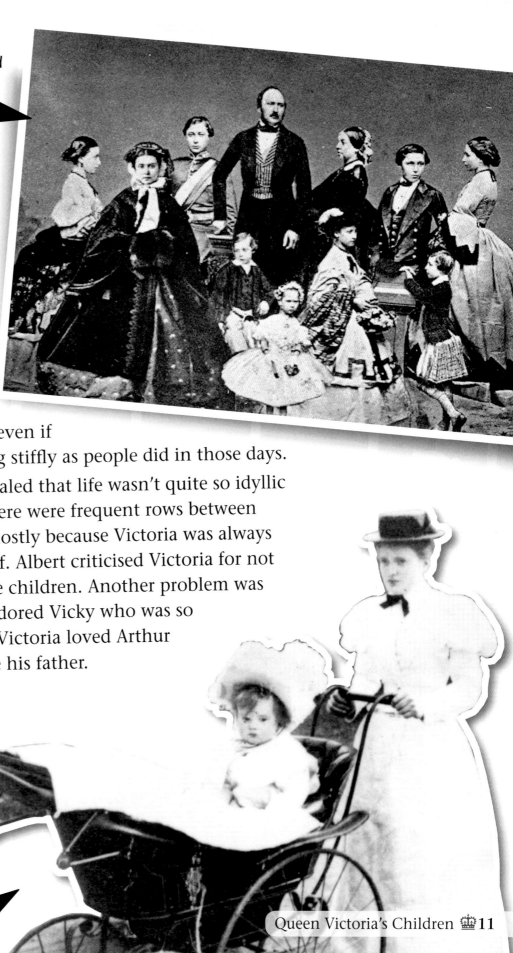

Queen Victoria and Prince Albert, surrounded by their children.

Family Snaps

The first photographs were taken in early Victorian times. The Royal Family had many loving portraits taken and helped to make it fashionable to have family snaps. Most of these pictures show an ideal family, even if its members are posing stiffly as people did in those days.

Historians have revealed that life wasn't quite so idyllic behind the scenes. There were frequent rows between Victoria and Albert, mostly because Victoria was always telling her children off. Albert criticised Victoria for not taking more joy in the children. Another problem was favouritism – Albert adored Vicky who was so bright and engaging. Victoria loved Arthur because he was so like his father.

Royal children were looked after by nannies, such as this one, from birth.

'Poor Bertie': Edward VII

The future Edward VII was born on 9 November 1841 at Buckingham Palace. He was christened Albert Edward, after his father. It was the first time in British history that the reigning queen had given birth to an heir so it was a big deal!

Albert Edward's birth had been difficult, probably because he was so big. It was the beginning of a stormy relationship between mother and son. In those days Queen Victoria preferred girls and called her new baby 'the boy'. To the rest of the family he became known as Bertie.

Terrible Tantrums

All eyes were on Bertie. He was going to be the King of England and Victoria and Albert set about grooming him for the role. When Bertie was seven, Albert devised a system of education for the boy.

An engraving showing Bertie as a child, rowing on the Thames at Windsor.

Bertie was born at Buckingham Palace in 1841. Today, the palace is still the official London residence of the monarch.

The trouble was, Bertie wasn't academic like his intelligent big sister, Vicky. Disappointed in their son, Bertie's father was strict with him and his mother was cruel, calling him lazy and backward. Bertie threw some terrible tantrums and in time developed a stammer.

Freedom At Last

Bertie tasted freedom for the first time when he was fourteen, on an official family visit to France. Bertie enjoyed the less rigid way of life there – there was dancing into the night and attractive French women smiled at him. It was much harder to return to his studies after that and soon afterwards he was allowed to go on walking tours and other visits without his parents.

Bertie was no great scholar but he grew into a charming, good natured and sociable character. Unfortunately, Bertie's parents never saw it that way and he was always made to feel inadequate.

Bertie Gets Booted and Suited

In later life Bertie was famous for his sense of style and sometimes changed his outfit six times a day! This was possibly a backlash against his childhood when he'd been made to wear clothes like kilts and sailor suits. When he was a teenager he was finally allowed to choose his own clothes but his mother did ask that they be neither 'too extravagant or slang'.

Bertie as a young man in military uniform.

The Second Son: George V

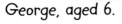

George, aged 6.

Bertie loved the ladies so Queen Victoria wanted him to be married off quickly. In 1863, at the age of 21, Bertie married beautiful eighteen-year-old Princess Alexandra of Denmark.

The following year they had their first son, Albert Victor, affectionately known as Eddy. Their second son, George, was born a year afterwards on 3 June 1865. George was third in line to the throne so it seemed unlikely that he would ever be king. Bertie and Alexandra were loving parents and went on to have more children: Louise, Victoria, Maud and Alexander John.

Prince Albert Victor – Eddy

George's older brother, known as Eddy, was eleven when this photo was taken. He died suddenly from influenza when he was 28. Some people think this is a good thing as Eddy was not as intelligent as his younger brother. He'd also been involved in a number of embarrassing scandals with very unsuitable girlfriends!

'Darling Mother Dear'

Bertie's own unhappy childhood didn't seem to stop him from being a good father. Alexandra was a maternal and caring mother who made regular appearances in the nursery at Sandringham. She wanted her boys to socialise with other children and have fun. She encouraged outdoor pursuits like horse riding and passed on her love of dogs. George adored his mother and called her 'Darling Mother Dear' all his life.

Sandringham House, a favourite royal residence.

Life at Sea

The young princes were educated together by tutors at home. Neither of the boys was academic but Bertie wasn't strict and wanted his sons to join the navy. In 1877 when George was twelve the boys enrolled as naval cadets in Dartmouth, Devon. George spent most of his teenage years at sea visiting parts of the British Empire. Queen Victoria did not approve of her grandson's career in the Royal Navy.

The future George V, dressed as a sailor.

The Royal Stamp Collection

George V has a reputation for being dull but in the world of stamp collecting he's a hero. Stamp collecting began when the first stamps were issued in 1840. George started collecting stamps as a child. In 1893 he was made the Honorary Vice President of the Royal Philatelic Society. Some of the stamps in George's collection are worth millions today.

The Shy Prince

George married Princess Mary of Teck in 1893 and became King George V in 1910. He had six children including the future kings, Edward VIII and George VI.

The childhood photographs of Albert Frederick, known as Bertie, who eventually became King George VI, show a slight blonde boy often wearing a sailor suit. In everyday life the future king was shy, sickly and knock-kneed with a stammer. Nobody ever expected him to be a king – all hopes were pinned on his big brother.

Life in the Shadows

Bertie's brother Edward (known as David in the family) was just a year older than him so they were raised and educated together. George V once said: "My father was scared of his father, I was scared of my father and I'm damned well going to see that they're scared of me." The boys spent most of their time with strict nannies.

Pictured here in a sailor suit, young Bertie, the future King George VI, went on to join the Royal Navy.

Bertie (left) and David (right), were close friends as children.

Navy Blues

In early childhood, Bertie had to wear splints to correct his knocked knees. He was also forced to write with his right hand, even though he was left-handed.

Life continued to be hard as a teenager. At 13 Bertie became a naval cadet and attended the Royal Naval College on the Isle of Wight. He was bullied and nicknamed the 'Sardine'. One time he was tied to a hammock and left screaming for help. He often came bottom of the class. At 17 he became a midshipman (junior officer) on HMS *Collingwood* where he was treated like the rest of the crew and slept in a hammock.

"Bertie is a delightful creature and we have so many interests in common."

Prince Edward

Bertie hoped to make a career in the Royal Navy.

The Lost Prince

The youngest son of George V and Queen Mary was called Prince John. He died aged 13 and is called the 'lost prince' because he was rarely mentioned. His story was made secret because he had epilepsy and possibly suffered from mental illness. At the age of 12 he was removed from Buckingham Palace to be raised separately by a nurse.

'Lilibet'

Bertie found love and happiness with his wife, Lady Elizabeth Bowes-Lyon. Their first child, Princess Elizabeth (Elizabeth Alexandra Mary), was born on 21 April 1926.

Her little sister, Princess Margaret, was born in 1930. Elizabeth was called 'Lilibet' by her family and the girls were affectionately known as 'the little princesses' everywhere they went.

A Normal Childhood

As royal childhoods go the little princesses had it pretty normal. Their homes in Windsor and London were homely and inviting and not particularly luxurious.

Bertie and Elizabeth were Duke and Duchess of York when this picture was taken.

Royal Reads

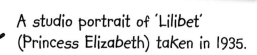

Dashing Uncle David, later briefly Edward VIII, loved visiting the little girls. He gave Elizabeth her treasured copies of A.A. Milne's *Winnie the Pooh* and *When We Were Young*, from which the girls learnt poems such as 'They are changing guard at Buckingham Palace'. *Black Beauty* by Anne Sewell and the *Doctor Dolittle* books were big favourites too.

A studio portrait of 'Lilibet' (Princess Elizabeth) taken in 1935.

The girls' parents joined in with games of hide-and-seek and pillow fights. Their father (now Duke of York) read them stories and their mother taught them to read. Yet, as was proper, the girls were raised by nannies and nurses and were taught by a governess.

Horse Play

Horses were a big part of Elizabeth's life. The Duke gave the girls a Shetland pony when Elizabeth was four. She also had a collection of toy horses that she fed, watered and unsaddled each day. Swimming was another passion and the sisters scooped certificates for life saving.

Family Scandal

In 1936, George V died and King Edward VIII took the throne. Later that year the Royal Family was scandalised when Edward abdicated. Lilibet's lovely world was about to change for ever...

Elizabeth loved dogs as a child and has kept pets all her life.

" She has an air of authority and reflectiveness astonishing in an infant. "

Winston Churchill describing Princess Elizabeth when she was two.

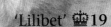

'Lilibet' 🜲19

Princess Elizabeth

Elizabeth's father suddenly became King George VI in 1936. The shy family man was unprepared for the job but it was his duty. The family moved to their grand new home – Buckingham Palace.

In fact, the palace was far too big and cold and it was like living in a museum. It took five minutes to reach the gardens. The Victorian nurseries and schoolrooms were dark and gloomy. The King insisted the girls' rooms be switched to the sunny side of the palace.

All Change

The little princesses had to get used to their parents going away on royal tours or performing royal duties. Most mornings the family made time to be together. The best times were the weekends when the family escaped back to the Royal Lodge at Windsor. There they could act like a normal family again, enjoying the outdoors and doing the gardening.

The Royal Family at the Royal Lodge, Windsor, in 1946. From left to right, King George VI, Princess Elizabeth, Princess Margaret, Queen Elizabeth.

Princess at War

Elizabeth was thirteen when the Second World War broke out in September 1939. The Royal Family decided to stay in London and brave the Blitz like everyone else. The princesses were issued with gas masks and lived on rations.

Elizabeth knew about current affairs and politics, and she wanted to do her bit for the war effort. When she reached the age of eighteen she eventually persuaded her father to let her volunteer with the Auxiliary Territorial Service (ATS). After the war ended, the princesses slipped out of the palace and mingled with the crowds to watch the celebrations.

Elizabeth trained as a driver and a mechanic during her time with the ATS.

Dressed in their Girl Guide uniforms in 1943, Elizabeth (left) is about to release a carrier pigeon while Margaret looks on.

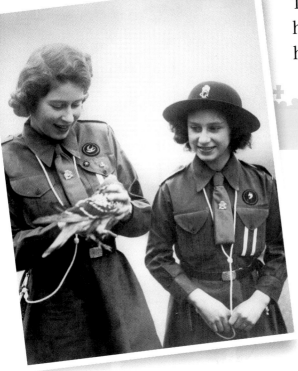

Princess Margaret

Elizabeth's sister, Margaret, was four years younger than her and the girls adored one another. Margaret was always more mischievous and fun loving than her sister. The girls' nanny, Crawfie, reckoned she could have been an actress, singer or dancer if she hadn't been a royal.

Plucky Girl Guides

At Buckingham Palace Elizabeth joined the Girl Guides and Margaret became a Brownie. Special Palace groups were set up with the children of Palace employees and court officials. It was the first time that royal children were encouraged to mix with other children.

Future King: Prince Charles

The Royal Family's decision to stay in London during the Second World War did wonders for its reputation. Royal fever hit again in 1947 when Princess Elizabeth married Philip Mountbatten. The arrival of their son, Prince Charles Philip Arthur George, on 14 November 1948 was another cause for celebration – the birth of a future king of England.

The future king and proud parents, pictured early in 1949.

Princess Anne was born two years later in 1950. There were no more royal babies until 1960 when Prince Andrew was born. Last in line is Prince Edward, born in 1964.

Bad Heir Days

Life isn't always easy for a future king. Big things are expected of you from the moment you're born. And constant royal duties mean that your parents are not around for you. As George VI's health deteriorated, Charles' parents were often away and on long tours abroad.

Charles was left in the care of his nannies and his grandmother whom he adored.

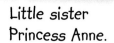

Little sister Princess Anne.

He grew into a shy, sensitive child with a love of being outdoors. In 1952 his grandfather died and his mother became Queen Elizabeth II. At the tender age of three Charles became second-in-line to the throne.

New School Rule

At first Charles was educated at home but when he was eight he was packed off to school, the first royal child to do so. He mixed with other children and joined the sports teams.

Later he went to a tough boarding school in Scotland called Gordonstoun. Prince Philip went there as a boy and thought it would do Charles good. Charles was unhappy there and called the place 'Colditz [after the Second World War German prisoner-of-war camp] in kilts'. He still managed to become Head Boy and left with six O-Levels and two A-Levels. Later he studied archaeology and anthropology at Trinity College, Cambridge.

Royal Spoiler Alert

The Royal Family don't believe in being extravagant with their gifts. When Charles wanted a new bicycle he didn't ask his parents as the answer was likely to be 'no'. Eventually, it was his great-uncle Lord Louis Mountbatten who gave him the bicycle as a combined Christmas and birthday present.

Off to school... Prince Charles, pictured in 1962 (far left), wearing a smart suit for his first term at Gordonstoun. Left, the Gordonstoun pipe band on parade.

The People's Prince: William

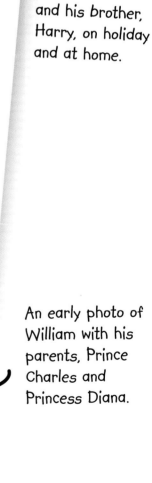

The popularity of the Royals hit an all-time high when Prince Charles married Lady Diana Spencer in July 1981. The crowds gathered outside Buckingham Palace again less than a year later when Prince William was born in 1982.

Life in the Spotlight

The childhood of this young royal was very different to his ancestors. Previous generations led mostly private lives behind closed palace doors. William has lived his life in the spotlight since the moment his parents stepped out of the hospital with him in their arms.

As he grew up, William was constantly photographed out and about with his mother and there were plenty of official photographs too.

Princess Diana enjoyed spending time with William and his brother, Harry, on holiday and at home.

An early photo of William with his parents, Prince Charles and Princess Diana.

Hands-on Parents

Diana loved children and had worked as a nanny and nursery assistant before marrying Charles. All parts of motherhood came naturally to her – from breast-feeding to changing nappies.

Charles was also a hands-on kind of father. He was regularly up in the nursery helping at bath time and giving baby William a bottle. When Charles and Diana went on a royal tour of Australia and New Zealand, nine-month-old William came too.

'Basher Wills'

William grew into a loud, mischievous child, nicknamed 'Basher Wills'. Diana wanted him to mix with children of his own age so William went to nursery and junior school, where he did well in class and sport. At thirteen William was sent to Eton College, where he gained twelve GCSEs and three A-levels. Next came St Andrew's University, where he met Kate Middleton, now his wife.

Kate Middleton met William at university.

Royal Commoner?

William grew up in the public eye (left, playing football at school). Meanwhile, his future wife Kate Middleton lived the life of a 'commoner'. Kate's parents worked for British Airways before forming a successful family business (her mother was a flight attendant, her father was a flight despatcher). Kate is the first commoner to marry an heir to the throne for over 350 years.

Party Prince: Harry

Prince Henry of Wales, better known as Prince Harry, was born on 15 September 1984. William and Harry have been called 'the heir and the spare' as Harry is third in line to the throne.

Charles and Diana's marriage was already in meltdown when Harry was born. The boys watched their parents arguing and their mother sulking. Harry was much shyer and clingier than his big brother. William was happy to go to school but when Harry went to nursery school it took him much longer to settle down.

Secret Treats

Diana and the boys often went out in disguise so that the boys could experience 'normal' life. A great afternoon out for the boys was made up of doing simple things like going to WH Smith to pore over comics and magazines. William and Harry also loved going to the cinema and tucking into burgers at McDonald's.

A Loving Mum

"I want my children to have as normal a life as possible... I hug my children to death and get into bed with them at night. I feed them love and affection."
Princess Diana

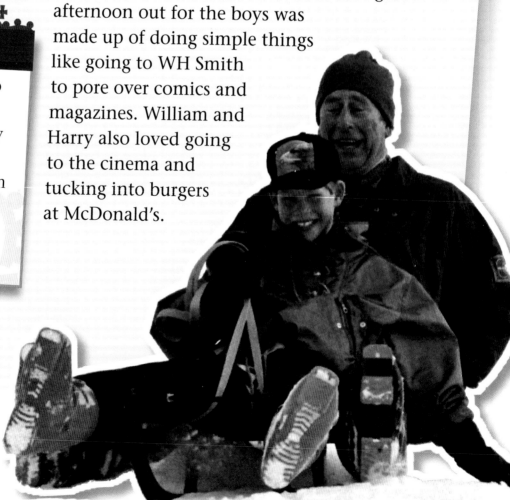

Charles enjoys an exciting toboggan ride with Harry.

Diana looks amused by Harry's boredom at this formal occasion.

'Hooray Harry'

Charles and Diana separated in 1992 and divorced in 1996. By then Harry had joined William at Eton. There, Harry shook off his shyness and started breaking the school rules, playing pranks on his friends or messing about. Later, he got a reputation for partying and having girlfriends. Harry regularly got low grades and longed to leave school but he still managed to scrape eleven GCSEs and two A-levels.

> " I want to carry on the things that she [Diana] didn't quite finish. I have always wanted to, but was too young. "
>
> Prince Harry on his 18th birthday

The Nation Mourns

Princess Diana died in a tragic car accident in Paris on 31 August 1997. People around the world were shocked and mourned her untimely death. William was fourteen and Harry was twelve when they lost their mother. The boys were devastated but did their royal duty and followed their mother's coffin during part of the funeral procession.

The funeral of Princess Diana. William and Harry walked behind the coffin, with their father, grandfather and uncle.

At his eighteenth birthday Harry told the press that he wanted to get involved in charity work: "I want to carry on the things that she [Diana] didn't quite finish. I have always wanted to, but was too young."

Life After Childhood

How did the monarchs of the past two hundred years grow and develop into their roles as rulers or heirs to the throne? Did their childhoods haunt them or give them the strength for the tough job ahead?

Prince Albert and Queen Victoria and their nine children.

Victoria and Son

Queen Victoria was young and inexperienced when she took the throne. She went on to rule for over 63 years, becoming the longest reigning queen in history. Being raised by her mother and nanny gave her the backbone to take charge and become one of history's most formidable monarchs.

Her son, Edward VII, did a good job of shaking off his childhood woes too. He had to wait until he was 59 before he became the King. By then he'd earned a reputation for being a ladies' man with a taste for gambling and night life. However, his liberal ways made him well liked and he was a good king.

Surviving the Scandal

Nautical George V was a strong leader through the dark days of the First World War.

Next came Edward VIII (David), the king that became famous for abdicating so he could marry his divorced lover, Wallis Simpson. The scandal rocked the

Edward VIII as a young man.

nation and meant his quiet shy brother George was forced to become King. Yet out of the ashes of royal scandal, George VI rose to become one of the most popular monarchs ever.

Elizabeth and 'the Firm'

Elizabeth II jokingly calls the Royal Family 'the Firm'. She has headed the family business for over sixty years. The Queen clung to her dignity during the scandal of Charles and Diana's divorce but lost popularity when Diana died by not appearing to be sympathetic. However, Diamond Jubilee celebrations in 2012 showed how much her people still admire her.

Meanwhile her son Charles, famous for his charity work and his green vision, has waited a lifetime to become King. Some people believe that his son William would be a better choice for our next monarch, but others are not so sure. With new royal children yet to be born, only one thing is clear: the monarchy will continue to evolve and change, as it has done for the past 200 years.

Three generations of royals enjoy time at Balmoral in Scotland: Prince Charles, his parents and grandparents.

William and his family

"We are all human and inevitably mistakes are made. But in the end there is a great sense of loyalty and dedication among the family and it rubs off on me. Ever since I was very small, it's something that's been very much impressed on me, in a good way."

Prince William on his 21st birthday

Glossary

Abdicate To give up the throne or position of power.

Academic Describes an intelligent person that enjoys learning and education.

Accede Take up an office or position, such as becoming the monarch of a country.

Ancestors People from whom you are descended; members of your family from a long time ago.

Auxiliary Territorial Service The woman's branch of the British Army created just before the Second World War.

Blitz The bombing of major British cities by the Germans during the Second World War; it gets its name from the German word 'Blitzkrieg' which means lightning war.

Charismatic Charming and popular with other people.

Comptroller A person employed to take charge of financial and official matters.

Commoner An ordinary citizen below the rank of peer (Lord or Lady).

Epilepsy A brain disorder that causes a person to have seizures and to pass out.

Gas masks Protective masks worn over the face to protect the wearer from poisonous gases.

Governess A woman employed by a household to educate the children.

Heir apparent The first person in line to the throne by birth.

Idyllic Perfect, beautiful and happy.

Influenza A viral infection that is easily passed between people and causes symptoms such as fever, aches and pains, weakness and exhaustion.

Liberal Describes a person who doesn't have traditional ideas and values. They are more open and willing to try new ways of doing things.

Nannies People employed to look after children in their own home.

Nautical To do with sailing or the sea.

Naval cadet A young trainee in the Royal Navy.

Private secretary A person employed to deal with the personal and public matters of a public figure such as a celebrity or monarch.

Privileged Describes a person with advantages such as wealth, position and power.

Regent A person that is appointed to make important official decisions if a monarch is still a child and too young to rule a country.

Scholar A person that is highly educated.

Stammer A difficulty with speaking clearly, characterised by breaks and pauses in speaking as well as repeating sounds and words.

Volunteer To offer to do a job for free.

Websites

http://www.royal.gov.uk
The official website for the British Royal Family. You can find out about the current Royal Family and their homes and duties. There is also a history of the British monarchy.

http://www.britroyals.com/
Find out lots of interesting facts about the history of the Royal Family as well as photographs, family trees and timelines.

http://www.queenvictoriasjournals.org/home.do
Investigate the journals of Queen Victoria for yourself on this website that went live during 2012, the year of Elizabeth II's Diamond Jubilee.

Note to parents and teachers

Every effort has been made by the Publishers to ensure that the web sites in this book are suitable for children, that they are of the highest educational value, and that they contain no inappropriate or offensive material. However, because of the nature of the Internet, it is impossible to guarantee that the contents of these sites will not be altered. We strongly advise that Internet access is supervised by a responsible adult.

Royal timeline

1819 Princess Victoria born

1837 Victoria becomes Queen

1840 Victoria marries Prince Albert

1841 Prince Albert Edward ('Bertie') born

1863 Bertie marries Princess Alexandra of Denmark

1865 Prince George born

1893 Prince George marries Princess Mary

1894 Prince Edward Albert ('David') born

1895 Prince Albert Frederick ('Bertie') born

1901 Queen Victoria dies and Prince Albert Edward becomes King Edward VII

1910 King Edward VII dies and Prince George becomes King George V

1923 Prince Albert Frederick marries Lady Elizabeth Bowes-Lyon

1926 Princess Elizabeth born

1936 King George V dies and Prince Edward Albert becomes King Edward VIII

1936 King Edward VIII abdicates and Prince Albert Frederick becomes King George VI

1952 King George VI dies and Princess Elizabeth becomes Queen Elizabeth II

1948 Prince Charles born

1981 Prince Charles marries Lady Diana Spencer

1982 Kate Middleton born; Prince William born

1984 Prince Harry born

1996 Prince Charles and Princess Diana divorce

1997 Princess Diana dies

2011 Prince William and Kate Middleton marry; they become the Duke and Duchess of Cambridge

Index

abdicate 5, 19
abdication 5, 19, 28
Auxiliary Territorial Service
    21

Balmoral 29
Bertie 10, 11, 12, 13 *see also*
    Edward VII
Bertie 16, 18, 19 *see also*
    George VI
Blitz 21
Bowes-Lyon, Lady Elizabeth
    18, 19 *see also* Queen
    Elizabeth
Buckingham Palace 9, 12, 17,
    18, 20, 21, 24

Churchill, Winston 19
Conroy, Sir John 6, 7, 8

Dash 7, 8
David 16, 17, 18, 28 *see also*
    Edward VIII
dogs 7, 8, 15, 19
Duchess of Kent 4, 6, 7, 8, 28
Duchess of York 5, 18, 19
    see also Queen Elizabeth
Duke of Kent 4, 6
Duke of York 5, 18, 19
    see also George VI

Eddy 14 *see* Prince Albert
    Victor
education 7, 12, 13, 15, 19,
    23, 25, 26, 27
Edward VII 4, 12–15, 28
Edward VIII 4, 5, 16, 18,
    19, 28
Eliot, George 10

Elizabeth II 4, 5, 8, 23, 29
    Diamond Jubilee 8, 29
    pets 19
    reading 18
Eton College 25, 27

First World War 28

George III 6
George IV 8
George V 4, 5, 14, 15, 16–19,
    28
George VI 4, 5, 16, 20, 22,
    23, 29
Girl Guides 21
Gordonstoun 23

horses 7, 15, 19

Kensington Palace 6, 7, 8, 9

Lehzen, Baroness Louise 7, 8

Middleton, Kate 25
Milne, A.A. 18
Mountbatten, Lord Louis 23

nannies 4, 11, 16, 19, 21, 22,
    25, 28

Prince Albert 4, 9, 10, 11, 12,
    13, 28
Prince Albert Victor 14
Prince Andrew 6, 22
Prince Arthur 10, 11
Prince Charles 5, 22–23, 24,
    25, 26, 27, 29
    divorce 26, 27, 29
Prince Edward 22
Prince Harry 24, 26–27

Prince John 17
Prince Philip 22, 23, 27, 29
Prince William 5, 24–25, 26,
    27, 29
Princess Alexandra 14, 15
Princess Anne 22
Princess Beatrice 6
Princess Diana 5, 24, 25, 26,
    27, 29
    death 27, 29
    divorce 26, 27, 29

Princess Elizabeth 18–21, 22,
    23 *see also* Elizabeth II
Princess Margaret 18, 20, 21
Princess Mary 16 *see also*
    Queen Mary
Princess Vicky 10, 11, 13
Princess Victoria 6–9 *see also*
    Queen Victoria

Queen Elizabeth 20, 22, 29
Queen Mary 4, 16, 17
Queen Victoria 4, 5, 9–13,
    14, 15, 28
    children 10–13, 28
    diary 8, 9
    reading 7

Royal Lodge 18, 20
Royal Navy 15, 16, 17, 28
Royal Stamp Collection 15

Sandringham House 15
Second World War 21, 22
Simpson, Wallis 28

William IV 8